Nursing Home Ministries

NURSING HOME MINISTRIES

by

Lola M. Williams

BEACON HILL PRESS OF KANSAS CITY
Kansas City, Missouri

Copyright, 1981
by Beacon Hill Press of Kansas City

ISBN: 0-8341-0710-4

Printed in the
United States of America

Cover design: Crandall Vail

Contents

Chapter 1

How to Start a Nursing Home Ministry

If you feel that you would like to minister to those in nursing homes, but do not quite know how to go about it, this little book is for you. Included are 12 sample lessons which you may use.

When you get ready to take on this project for the Lord, talk with your pastor about it. He will probably be glad to help you get started. Ask him to have the church board appoint you. Then ask that he announce it in the church bulletin and from the pulpit, so people will understand that this is your responsibility. Also, be bold in asking that the church board enlist some helpers for you; but if there are none forthcoming, do not be afraid to go alone. The important thing is that you care enough to go, then do it.

Visit the nursing home in person where you wish to have services. Talk to the administrator in charge. Tell the staff your intentions. Ask their cooperation. Inquire about songbooks, a place to meet, and the best time for services. Morning, afternoon, or evening will do; but plan it so it will not be too close to meals, naps, or bedtime. The administrator can give you this information.

Set up a starting date soon. Many of the residents of nursing homes do not have a long time to wait. Plan to have your meeting regularly so they can depend on you. You may have it once a week, twice a month, or once a month. Most nursing home personnel are happy for church groups to have services for the residents, and will gladly include it in a calendar of events.

Before having your first meeting, visit with as many of the residents of the nursing home as possible. Find out their names and tell them yours. Win their friendship, and they'll look forward eagerly to attending your meetings.

If you absolutely cannot be there when they expect you, try to get a substitute. They will feel let down if someone doesn't come. If no one is able to go, call the nursing home as early as you can so the residents will not be left waiting.

Trying to make them over to your particular denomination will only cause heartache. They come from many religious backgrounds, and they will actively resist change. They will, however, appreciate you ministering to them in the name of Jesus Christ.

If you teach them a Bible lesson each time you meet, you may count them as an outreach class for your Sunday School. That's exactly what you will be doing, reaching out to them in the love of Jesus. Do your counting discreetly. No one enjoys being a mere statistic.

Many times these people are the forgotten ones of society. When you minister to them, they will rise up (at least emotionally if not physically) and call you blessed.

The overworked staff of the home will appreciate your interest in their patients. They deal firsthand with the loneliness and boredom these people experience each day.

They know that food, clothing, and shelter are not enough. The oil of love helps to make the rough spots of life a little smoother.

Most of all, the Lord himself will bless you for your efforts. "Inasmuch as ye have done it unto one of the least of these my brethren, ye have done it unto me" (Matt. 25:40).

Chapter 2

What to Expect in a Typical Nursing Home

Nursing home residents have been removed from the mainstream of life. They are not in complete control of their personal business anymore. They no longer maintain their own homes, rear families, pay taxes, plan their own meals, or regulate their own comings and goings. This is all behind them. In some cases, where mental retardation is present, they have never enjoyed these privileges of life.

They are not always elderly. Some, in fact, may be quite young, in their early adult years, teen years, or even childhood. These are the ones who were born physically deformed or mentally handicapped, or both. Some may be there because they have illnesses that demand constant attention, yet they do not need to be hospitalized.

Either their families cannot or, in some cases, will not care for them at home. Some may have no living relatives.

People in nursing homes are sick, lonely, discouraged, and many times impoverished. They may be facing imminent death, looking back on life instead of forward.

Their attention span is short like a small child's.

They are childlike in many other ways also. While you try to minister to them, some will sleep (even snore loudly), some will cry, some will look off into their own faraway world, and some will interrupt you. Some may talk continuously either to themselves or their neighbor, while you are presenting the lesson. Others will be surprisingly alert and hang onto your every word.

Many times they will not be too pleasant to be near. They may belch in your face, vomit, or wet all over themselves. Try to remember, they don't want to be this way. They are not purposely being rude or crude. They would give almost anything to be physically whole and attractive persons leading active lives. A little genuine Christlike love will go a long way.

Some will be devout Christians, some will be openly cynical, and others will seem to be indifferent. But they are all human beings for whom Christ died.

Some of the nursing homes will be clean, modern, and well staffed, with excellent equipment. Others may be understaffed, hot, stuffy, smelly, and not too clean. Their equipment will be inadequate or nonexistent. Learn to adapt to the circumstances without criticism. You are there to bring a little sunshine to their lives through loving concern and presenting God's Word in a winning way.

You do not need stylish clothes, a fancy car, a large bankroll, an impressive family tree, or even a lot of education to minister to these needy people. All you really need is an extra measure of love, patience, and understanding.

Listen to their problems, but don't burden them with yours. They can't handle it. This will only serve to upset them.

Take time out to shake hands with them, perhaps pat their workworn hands, smile, and bring a cheery word or two. It costs you nothing but a little of your time, and it will mean a lot to them.

Ministry Through Music, Caring, and Gifts

Once in a while, it would be good to have some special singers to present a musical program for the nursing home residents. They may be hungering to hear some good gospel music.

Older people especially enjoy seeing young people. The younger residents of the home will also appreciate seeing other young people. On some occasions, take a group of teens from your church to sing for them or play their musical instruments. These people will not expect perfection; they only want a little attention.

It will have the added bonus of giving the teens a service project. They will also have opportunity to see how those less fortunate ones must live.

Some nursing homes will have hymnals available. Other places you may have to carry them with you each time. Perhaps your church would be willing to donate several hymnals to the home.

Remember, they will almost always prefer the old, familiar hymns, because they can sing along without a book. Some of them can't see well enough to read now, so they cling to the hymns they recognize. The books for their use should have big enough print for them to read easily.

Some nursing home residents will be able-bodied enough to come to an occasional service at your home church, if transportation is provided. Check with those in charge to make sure this is allowed before suggesting it.

A special service of recognition for the nursing home residents might be held at the church on a Sunday morning. Several people from the church might be willing to bring these people in their cars. Perhaps a church bus could be used.

One church has a special meal once a month for those nursing home residents who are able to get out occasionally. The teens from the church who have their driver's licenses act as chauffeurs and bring the eager guests to the church's fellowship hall. No need to caution the teens to drive carefully. They are so pleased to be trusted with such an important mission, they drive their very best.

Once the guests are seated, the teens help serve them the meal, which has been furnished and cooked by several church families. At the close of the meal, a special program is presented for the guests. Then their young drivers take them back to the home. Afterwards, the teens return to the fellowship hall, where they help wash dishes, etc.

Some of the residents might enjoy just going for a ride in the country, or past their old neighborhoods, if they happen to be nearby. A brief outing to a park close to the home would give them a change of scenery.

A lady once visited a nursing home unannounced, in the middle of the day, to see her mother. She was surprised to see several of the residents all dressed up as though they were going out.

She asked the nurse, "Are they going somewhere today?"

"Oh, no," came the reply. "They never have any-where to go, so each afternoon they get all dressed up in their best clothes and pretend that someone is coming to take them on an outing."

How sad. These once active members of society must now play little games of pretense with themselves in order to get any pleasure from life.

Some nursing homes have handcraft times for the residents. Sometimes the ladies enjoy making lap quilts, aprons, potholders, or other small items from scraps of new material. Ask the women of your church who sew to save their scraps, trimming the ragged edges for easier handling. Then, when you've collected a bagful, take them to your favorite nursing home.

On special occasions, it would be nice to give them little gifts. Some of these occasions might be Christmas, Thanksgiving, Easter, and other holidays. Be careful about giving candy. Many will be diabetic and should not have it, though they may eagerly reach for it. Better check with the administrator to see what the residents can or cannot eat.

A decorated egg at Easter time would brighten their day and cost little. Some little Christmas favor would be appreciated by them. It need not be elaborate or expensive. Some of them may have no family to bring them gifts. Your thoughtfulness will mean so much to them.

Before giving gifts, check at the office of the nursing home for some gift suggestions. They will probably be glad to help.

Here are a few gift ideas: hankies for both men and women; illustrated books of poetry in large print; small religious pictures or plaques they can set near their beds; big print New Testaments; a small plant that does not require a lot of care; combs; talcum powder; sweet-smelling soap; stationery and postage stamps; sachets; book markers; or little boxes of raisins.

At Christmastime, if your church would be willing to take on the added time and expense to give bigger gifts, here are some things that could be given: Some of the ladies from the church might knit or crochet sweaters, shawls, or lap afghans; pretty little aprons or house slippers with nonskid soles would be appreciated.

The greatest gift you can give, of course, is yourself. The gift of your time, your caring, and your smile will always be acceptable and in order.

Chapter 4

How to Lead Them to Christ

People can still be saved in the "eleventh hour" of their lives. Even if only a few are made ready for heaven over several years of work, it will be well worth the effort.

As was mentioned earlier, some will already be Christians. Others may seem unable to understand about salvation, or they may not wish to embrace Christianity. No matter how much you may want them to be saved, it has to be their own decision.

Some will just be waiting for you to lead them to Christ. Perhaps they've been a Christian at some time in their lives, and now are afraid it's too late to come back to God. Others may have put off their salvation, always waiting for that convenient time that never seems to come.

Some lessons will easily lend themselves to a gentle evangelistic appeal. Other times, you may feel it is the right time to present Jesus Christ to them individually.

Do not be afraid. If you love the Lord yourself, then you can lead others to Him. Do not put it off until the pastor can come and pray with them. The opportune time may have passed by then, or they may have already slipped into eternity unprepared.

If you have never taken a course on personal evangelism, you can still use this simple A-B-C method to lead another to Christ.

Speak gently, but do not allow them to despair. Even if they have rejected Christ all of their lives, it is still not too late to seek and find Him now.

Here are the ABCs of salvation, which you may present to them.

A. Admit you are a sinner. "For all have sinned, and come short of the glory of God" (Rom. 3:23).

B. Believe, not only in the existence of Jesus, but that He can and will save you. "Believe on the Lord Jesus Christ, and thou shalt be saved" (Acts 16:31).

C. Confess your sins to Jesus. "If we confess our sins, he is faithful and just to forgive us our sins, and to cleanse us from all unrighteousness" (1 John 1:9).

They may not know how to pray. You may have to pray a simple prayer of repentance with them, asking them to repeat it word for word after you. They need not list all the sins they've committed in a lifetime. That would be impossible. They only need to *admit* their need, *believe* Jesus will save them, and *confess* their sins to Him; that is, to tell Him they are sorry for their sins, and ask to be forgiven.

If they have done all these steps, tell them they have the right to believe that Jesus saves them. Some will show a lot of emotion, others may not seem to be any different outwardly. It's what is in the heart that counts.

After they have confessed their faith, pray for them, right then, that God will help them keep their faith, even through the trying times which come to all Christians. Offer them the beautiful hope of heaven without pain, death, sickness, or sorrow.

Check on them as often as possible, to see how they are coming spiritually. In a sense, you will become their pastor. Let them lean on you for encouragement.

At times, your work will get you down. You may be tempted to not even try.

Two scriptures that will gird you up when you falter are: "And let us not be weary in well doing: for in due season we shall reap, if we faint not" (Gal. 6:9); and, "Joy shall be in heaven over one sinner that repenteth" (Luke 15:7).

May God bless you as you endeavor to bring the lost ones to Jesus. You have nothing to lose and everything to gain for your efforts.

Chapter 5

How to Conduct a Nursing Home Service

A nursing home service should last no more than 30 minutes. Your meetings will consist mainly of singing congregational hymns (the old familiar ones); praying for and with the people, sometimes using the Lord's Prayer; and a Bible lesson each time.

You will not be using time for offering and announcements. Probably, you will not have special music every service, either. Too long a service only wears out the people.

It is advisable, when reading scripture, to use only the King James Version. That is the Bible they grew up with and reared their families by. They do not readily accept the new translations, however good these may be elsewhere.

They resist change of any kind. If you make an issue of translations, you will upset them and weaken your own effectiveness for Christ.

Many of these people have been uprooted from their homes and families. They have already had many adjustments to make. Allow them the privilege of having a Bible they can be familiar with. Millions of people have found the way to heaven through the King James Version, and these people can also.

It would be worthwhile to purchase, or have the church to purchase, one or more books of poetry for your use. Nursing home residents enjoy poetry so much they will sometimes ask for a copy of a particular poem for themselves. These books of poetry can be used over and over. These lonely ones do not mind repetition. Even though you may feel you do not read poetry well, make an effort. They will love you for it. It is a good idea to use at least one poem each service.

Large teaching pictures, such as those used for teaching children, could be used to illustrate various lessons. Again, they could be used over and over. We all remember more of what we see than what we only hear. This is why television became so popular over radio.

Always let them see you reading the scripture from the Bible even if you know it from memory. This way they are sure it really is God's Word, and not just yours. Some of them may repeat the scripture along with you, if it is a familiar passage.

Any Bible-based theme is all right to have a lesson on, but some are more appropriate than others. Keep the scripture reading brief, or their attention will wane.

Lessons from the Psalms are always suitable. Old Testament stories of action are well received. Do not be afraid to be dramatic if you are a good storyteller. They will follow you as eagerly as children. New Testament stories about Jesus, the disciples after Pentecost, and stories from the life of Paul are always enjoyed.

Better take it easy on subjects such as water baptism and Communion. These are things most of them can no longer participate in. Too much said about them may leave the people feeling frustrated. Also, do not rely heavily on the miracles of healing for your lessons. It would be hurtful to hold out false hopes to them. God heals the body of many physical afflictions, but He does not choose to heal from old age.

Keep the lessons short and simple. Their attention span is not very long. Ten to 15 minutes is long enough for the Bible lesson. Be careful about using "churchy" language. If they have not been regular church attenders, they will not know what you mean.

When singing, allow them to choose the songs often. They will have their favorites, which they will sing with enthusiasm if not always on key.

If you have a piano player, well and good; but if not, you can sing without accompaniment. Even if you are not a great singer, smile like you enjoy it, and sing from your heart. They will not be critical.

I have included 12 sample lessons. You may use these as they are. Also, you might wish to use them to help you to know how to prepare future lessons. Each lesson is written in simple language to make them easy to understand. They are meant to be used as a guide rather than being read to the people.

Always close the service with a prayer that offers hope. When the service is over, try to linger for a few minutes to visit with them as one friend to another. If you rush out the door as if to say, "Well, that's over for a while and I'm glad," they will be hurt. It already seems to them that the world is rushing by without taking time to notice them. Don't let them feel that way about God's people, too.

It may be your responsibility to conduct regular classes at a nursing home, or only give an occasional lesson. Whatever your situation, my prayer is that this book will make your job easier and more pleasant for both teacher and pupils.

The Garden of the Heart

Did any of you ever have a garden? Remember how hard you worked planting it just so? Then later you took such care to keep it watered. When the tender plants began to break through the ground, the weeds came up, too. Then you probably spent many long, backbreaking hours pulling those weeds so your vegetables or flowers could grow unhindered.

A lady decided to plant a flower garden next to her house, but she didn't know much about gardens. She wanted something easy to plant that took very little care. After looking over different packages of flower seeds, she finally selected one that just read "Surprise Package."

She planted them and settled back to wait for her beautiful garden to bloom. She got her surprise, all right. The only thing that grew in her garden was a riot of ugly weeds. Perhaps if she had been more careful in her selection and worked harder at it, she might have been rewarded with the garden she had dreamed of.

In an area where there are a lot of farms, the TV commercials will outdo themselves to tell us how this or that weed killer is the best one to use on our crops. They will name all the various kinds of weeds their particular brand will eliminate.

Our hearts are like gardens, too. We need to have them planted with the seeds of love. Not just any seeds will do. In order to have a good harvest, we need to have our hearts planted with the seeds of God's love.

If we're not careful, weeds will spring up and choke out the love that has been so carefully planted. Some of the weeds that can choke out God's love are bitterness, anger, hatred, misunderstanding, and selfishness.

Gardens can be things of great beauty. The Garden of Eden surely was. God went there to walk and talk with Adam and Eve.

Our hearts can be like gardens where God will commune with us. The chorus of the old, familiar hymn "In the Garden" goes:

And He walks with me, and He talks with me,
And He tells me I am His own;
And the joy we share as we tarry there,
None other has ever known.

The Bible tells us some of the fruits of the Spirit-filled life are joy, peace, kindness, patience, long-suffering, and love. Those fruits are worth cultivating, aren't they?

Some of you may be able to look out your window and see a garden that is planted nearby. If it is a garden that is well taken care of, it brings pleasure to all who see it.

If the gardens of our hearts are well taken care of, our lives will bring pleasure to others, our families, friends, roommates, and even those who take care of us.

* * *

Close by praying for each one present, that their hearts will be like a beautiful garden where God can come and walk and talk with them, and give them joy in their lives.

SCRIPTURE: *Judg. 5:1-3*

God Uses a Lady Judge

This is a part of a song of praise to God that Deborah and Barak sang after the battle was over and victory was theirs. Instead of trying to claim credit for the victory, they gave praise to God for deliverance.

The people of Israel had turned their backs on God and were worshipping idols. He punished them by allowing a wicked king from another country to oppress and rule over them for about 20 years. Finally the people repented of their sins and cried out to God to save them from their enemies.

God heard their prayers. He chose to send their deliverance through a woman named Deborah. She had been serving God right along, while many others had turned away from Him. In a time when there was great prejudice against women as leaders, this lady was well thought of and respected.

Deborah was a lady judge and a prophetess. She had the same authority as a man judge had in that time. As a prophetess, she foretold future events which God revealed to her. She was given the same respect a man prophet would have been given. Deborah did these things because God called her to do them and equipped her for the tasks.

Under God's direction, she contacted Barak, a great soldier. He was to gather an army of 10,000 men, and God would lead them to victory. This sounds like a lot of soldiers, but the enemy had many more.

Recognizing that God was using Deborah, Barak requested that she go with the army. Perhaps he felt her godly presence would assure victory.

When William Booth, the founder of the Salvation Army, died, his daughter Evangeline became its leader. Under her guidance the Salvation Army grew tremendously and became a strong champion of the "down and out" person of the streets.

God does not call every woman of God to be a Deborah or an Evangeline Booth; but He will use, in some way, everyone who serves Him—man, woman, or child. One such servant of God was a lady from a small country church. She never traveled far from home, never led an army, never wrote a book, and never held a public office. She devoted her life to her husband and seven children, being a good neighbor, working in church, and praying.

Yet, when she died, traffic was backed up for blocks around the funeral home. People had to stand in line to pay their respects. Story after story came out about how she had taken hot food to sick neighbors, cared for their children, and even cleaned their houses until they were well again. Some told of watching her year after year, as she trudged down the road to church with Bible in hand. Her Sunday School pupils over the years felt her godly influence on their lives.

If you have served God faithfully through the years, do not feel that you have done nothing for His kingdom. Your influence will be felt in lives for many years, in some areas you may not have even been aware of.

*   *   *

Close in prayer by thanking God for the faithful believers who have served Him where they were needed over the years.

Scripture: *1 Sam. 1:10-17*

Hannah, a Dedicated Mother

Hannah was sad because she had no children. Being a God-fearing woman, she knew just what to do. She prayed for a child and promised the Lord she would give him back to God. God heard her prayer and gave her a healthy son, whom she named Samuel.

True to her word, when he was still a very small boy, she took him to the house of the Lord and dedicated him to God. Then she left him there to assist the priest, Eli. Samuel grew up in the house of God. His mother loved him very much, but she kept her vow to God. Samuel grew up to be one of God's greatest prophets. Perhaps part of the reason was because of the unselfish dedication of his mother, Hannah.

Eventually, Hannah and her husband were blessed with other children who were permitted to stay in the home until they grew to adulthood. Each year she would make the boy, Samuel, a new suit of clothes and take it to him, but she never took back her promise to God. She knew that the first duty of a mother is to bring that child up to serve God.

Most of you can remember your own mothers. You have precious memories of them working to cook delicious meals, mend the clothes, clean the house, nurse the little childish hurts, and many other things. Probably a number of you are mothers yourselves. You can recall doing things for your families because you loved them. A loving mother works long and hard and asks little or nothing in return.

Mothers have always wanted the best for their children. When there was sickness in the home, it was usually Mother who nursed the sick one back to health. It is hard to stand by and watch our loved ones suffer, either from sickness or some injustice to them. A mother would almost always rather have the sickness or unjust treatment herself than have her child bear it. Yet, one of the jobs of a mother is to teach her child to cope with life's hurts when they do come.

A pastor of a certain church once had a contest to see who would be voted "Mother of the Year" in his church. For several weeks, every person that came to church was allowed to vote for the mother of their choice. When the contest ended and the votes were counted, a fine lady had been named "Mother of the Year." The pastor and others in the church said many nice things about this special mother and gave her the honor she was due.

Then the pastor called his own wife to stand by his side. He took her hands in his and told the congregation, "When I married my wife, her hands were soft and smooth. Now they are rough and calloused, but to me they are the most beautiful hands in the world, because they are the hands of a loving mother. She has worked hard caring for me and our six children."

Someone suggested, "God couldn't be everywhere, so He made mothers." Of course, we know God *can* be everywhere, but He still made mothers to give that loving touch that no one else can quite duplicate. For many of us, now, we have only tender memories of our mothers, but we can be thankful for the blessing of memory.

*   *   *

Close by praying a prayer of thanks that the world has been a better place to live because of the loving sacrifices of mothers everywhere.

Scripture: *1 Sam. 10:17-26*

The People Would Not Listen

Samuel the prophet was getting old. He had followed God's guidance in leading the people of Israel, but now they were unhappy. They wanted a king.

Samuel was hurt and bewildered. He tried to warn the people of the dangers of having a king. They would be forced to pay heavy taxes to the king. He would draft their choice young men into his army. Sometime in the future, a wicked king might even lead the people away from God.

The people would not listen. They were determined to have their own way, so God instructed Samuel to go ahead and give them a king. They were not rebelling against Samuel; they were rebelling against God.

Some of the reasons why they thought they needed a king were: fear of their enemies; they were unhappy with Samuel's sons; and they wanted to be like other nations. They thought if they had a king, he would go out and fight their battles for them.

Samuel was a God-fearing man who had led the people well, but his sons, who would be the leaders after his death, were not like him. They were corrupt men, taking bribes and giving out unfair judgments against the people.

Other nations around them had kings, so they thought they wanted to be like their neighbors. God wanted to lead their government directly, but they had made up their minds to have a king. Have you ever heard a child declare,

"But Mom, all the other kids have one." Children want to be just like the other kids. The people of Israel were like children. The other nations had kings, so they wanted a king also.

Sometimes when we insist on a certain thing, God permits us to have our wishes, but we have to live with the mistakes we make. God permitted the people of Israel to have their king. A young man named Saul was chosen. The first thing he did was run and hide. Perhaps he was afraid of the great responsibilities of being king. Perhaps he preferred to remain an ordinary citizen.

Whatever his reasons, God told Samuel where Saul was hiding. He was brought out and presented to the people as their king. They were well pleased with Saul and shouted, "God save the king."

Down through the years after that time, the people of Israel had a number of kings. Some were good rulers, leading the people in the ways of God. Others were wicked men who led the people into idol worship. The predictions Samuel had made about having a king all came true.

Even in the good times, they had to take second best. Being ruled by a king, even a good one, is not nearly as satisfying as being led directly by God.

Possibly some of you, in years past, did not follow the way God tried to lead you. Because of insisting on having your own way, your lives may not have been as satisfying as they might have been.

You cannot undo the mistakes of the past, but you can ask for God's guidance for the rest of your lives. He still wants to lead you just as He wanted to lead the people of Israel back in Samuel's day.

*   *   *

Close in prayer by asking God to guide each one of us, helping us to make the right choices for the rest of our lives.

29

SCRIPTURE: *2 Kings 2:9-15*

The Young Learn from the Old

Elijah the prophet was old. Soon he would be going to heaven. For some time, a young man named Elisha had been his constant companion. This young man was the one God had chosen to be the next great prophet.

There was a strong bond of love between the two men, almost like a father and son relationship. Elisha was already a God-fearing young man, but probably he learned a lot more from Elijah about trusting God.

Picture in your minds how these two worked together every day, with Elisha listening eagerly to the stories Elijah told of the miracles of God. There was the time the ravens brought bread and meat every morning to Elijah so he would not starve. God always takes care of His own.

Possibly he told Elisha about the time on Mount Carmel when 450 prophets of the idol Baal had prayed all day for their god to send fire to consume the sacrifice on the altar. Then when Elijah prayed one short prayer to the real God, fire came down from heaven and consumed the altar and everything on or around it. God never does things in a small way.

Now Elijah would soon be leaving the young prophet whom he had grown to love. He asked the younger man to name one last thing he could do for him before going to heaven. Elisha did not hesitate to make his request known. He wanted his ministry to be blessed of God as Elijah's had been.

The older prophet did not have the authority to grant such a request. He did, however, tell Elisha that if he saw Elijah being taken to heaven, then his request would be granted.

Soon a chariot of fire came down and transported Elijah to heaven. Elisha saw it and cried out, "My father, my father." His great friend and teacher was gone. It would be up to him to carry on God's work.

A number of years ago, a minister was about to retire. He had enjoyed a long and fruitful ministry for God and was about to step down and take a well-earned rest. He had three sons in the ministry. Someone remarked that he had left quite a heritage to the younger generation. He replied that he had also received quite a heritage. For over 400 years, without a break, there had been ministers in this man's family.

God was the one who called these into the ministry, but it was in their homes and from their godly parents they had first become aware of a need to know God in a personal way. Each generation impressed this need upon the next.

In all areas of life, places of leadership must be passed on to the next generation. In the years to come, they, too, will step down for the future generations. This is the way God planned it.

We can probably all remember the sound advice and help we received from the generation before us. Then, later, it became our turn to pass on the reins of leadership to the younger ones.

The greatest heritage we can leave the younger generation is the sound advice to seek God early in their lives.

If we can do this, then in the eyes of God, we have been successful in life no matter what the world may think of us.

*   *   *

Close in prayer by thanking God for the wonderful heritage left us by those saints who have gone on before us.

SCRIPTURE: *Ps. 5:1-3, 11-12*

Prayer in the Morning

David was the king, the ruler of a nation, yet he felt the need to pray. He declares that every morning he will pray, before he takes on the duties of the day.

A certain lady was in the habit of rising early and spending time in prayer and Bible reading to begin her day. Then, after a light breakfast, she would read the newspaper before she left for work.

One morning, the alarm did not go off and she overslept. She could tell at a glance that she wouldn't have time for everything. She knelt by her bed to ask God's guidance for the day. Then she hurriedly dressed for work. She still had 15 minutes to spare before she must leave. She had read neither her Bible nor her newspaper. The devil whispered to her, "Read the newspaper first. You can read your Bible when you get home from work."

She hesitated only a second, then picked up her Bible and read it instead. She felt that reading God's Word was more vital to her day than reading about the day's happenings in the world.

In the psalm we read earlier, David sought divine guidance in the morning. Then he went out to meet the enemies of that day, assured that God would help him defeat them. He had no doubt in his heart that he would receive the help he asked for.

David put his days in the right order. The first thing he did was worship God through morning prayer. That fortified him for the rest of the day. The next thing he did was arrange or plan his day, confident that God would guide him. The last part was to watch for the enemy, that is, the temptations, discouragements, and lonely times. They'll show up as regularly as the sunrise and sunset. Prayer in the morning will help you through these bad times.

If you are no longer physically able to kneel to pray, God understands. You can pray in your bed before you get up, or perhaps sit up on the edge of your bed to pray before you get dressed.

If you are afraid that praying out loud will disturb your roommates, pray silently. God hears our prayers whether they are spoken out loud or prayed only in our hearts.

Prayer in the morning draws us closer to God all day long. It fortifies us for everything that comes our way that day. It helps us to be kinder and more patient with others. When we fail to start with prayer, a vital part of our day is missing.

To be able to pray is a privilege. It doesn't matter what our age, sex, physical condition, or finances are, we can all enjoy the wonderful privilege of prayer every day.

*   *   *

Close by leading everyone in the Lord's Prayer.

SCRIPTURE: *Ps. 34:1-8*

Song of Deliverance

This psalm is one of the best-loved psalms of all. It is often called a song of deliverance from fear, danger, trouble, and affliction.

God does not promise we will never experience these things. As long as we live on earth, we'll have troubles. He does promise that He will save us out of them. He will either make a way of escape or give us the grace and strength to go through them.

David starts out this psalm in much the same way as he starts several others, by praising the Lord for His goodness. Then he tells how, in times of trouble, he cried out to the Lord, who heard him and gave him deliverance.

The story is told of an elderly black man who had formerly been a slave but was now free after the Civil War. Years later, he visited Lincoln's tomb. Tourists came, climbed the steps leading up to the statue of Lincoln, glanced at it curiously, then left. This man stayed a long time, gazing up at the stone image of the great man. Someone noticed the black man had tears in his eyes, and asked what was the matter. Without shifting his gaze from the statue, the black man replied, "To some, Mr. Lincoln was a troublemaker. To others he was a good president of our country. To me, he is my emancipator. He delivered me from the bonds of slavery."

The human race views God in different ways. Some people act like they don't believe God even exists. They go muddling through life carrying all their fears, troubles, and afflictions themselves, and being broken by the heavy load.

Others consider God as a kindly "old man upstairs" who looks down on us in pity. Yet, according to their thinking, God is too weak to help us.

Born-again Christians have learned, with the Psalmist, that when they seek the Lord, He will deliver them from fears and save them out of their troubles. All of us have fears at times, but some people never seem to find deliverance.

A certain lady spent all of her waking hours in worry. Her husband was a truck driver; she just knew he'd have a wreck. Some terrible calamity would overtake her married children or grandchildren, even though they all lived nearby, and she could see they were all right.

She worried about the weather, but her worrying did not change a thing. She worried about money, but her husband had a good job, and they didn't owe a penny to anyone.

One day her husband grew tired of her constant worrying. He told her, "If you didn't have anything to worry about, you'd worry because you had nothing to worry about."

This lady, while a Christian, was not a very effective one. She was so caught up in her worrying she had little time or energy for anything else.

She had never taken this fourth verse seriously. In it, David gave us the secret when he wrote, "I sought the Lord, and he heard me, and delivered me from all my fears."

* * *

Close by praying that God will deliver us from our fears and help us to trust Him more.

Scripture: *Psalm 67*

"Let the People Praise Thee"

When someone does something that benefits all mankind, people praise that person because they are grateful for the good thing which has been done. Wise parents praise a child for being good, as well as chiding him when he has been bad. Everyone appreciates sincere praise for a job well done.

God wants our praise, too. This psalm is a song of praise to God. All of God's people should praise Him daily for all the benefits He sends us.

This psalm was written for the Jewish people, but we can all learn from it. They are God's chosen people, not because they are better than other people, but because they were to share with the whole world the story of the true and living God.

The Psalmist knew that if God's people did their job right, God's way would be known all over the world, and salvation would spread to all nations. He is praising God for this wonderful privilege.

Have you ever watched people walking down the street? Some will shuffle along, looking down at the street, and seem to be very unhappy. Others will have a grim look on their faces that says life hasn't been very pleasant for them. A little child may skip happily on his way as though he hadn't a care in the world. Once in a while, you'll see someone walking along who has a happy smile on his face. You wonder what good thing has happened to this person, and almost wish they would share it with you.

Christians should be happy people, praising God often for His goodness. We can praise the Lord with our words, by our actions, and by the expressions on our faces. We may be praising the Lord in our hearts, but if it doesn't show on our faces, how will anyone know?

A certain lady was known to often say, "Well, praise the Lord." She praised God for allowing her to live another day. She praised Him for the food she ate. She praised Him for the sunshine and the rain, the heat and the cold. She praised Him for providing a home for her. She praised Him for her church. She praised Him for the boys and girls in her Sunday School class. People grew accustomed to her constantly praising the Lord.

One day one of her grandsons knew that something unpleasant had just happened to her. He was amazed to hear his grandma say, "Well, praise the Lord."

The little boy asked, "Grandma, why are you praising the Lord? That was not something good."

His grandma was quick to reply, "I know it wasn't, but I'll praise the Lord anyway. It might have been worse."

It's easy to give praise to God when everything is going good. It's much harder to give praise when the bad times come. Yet the Psalmist says, "Let the people praise thee, O God; let all the people praise thee." Then the psalm closes with a promise: "God shall bless us; and all the ends of the earth shall fear him."

We can praise God in the morning, at noon, or at night. Anytime is the right time for God's people to give Him praise.

*   *   *

Close with prayer. Give praise to God for all His goodness to us.

Scripture: *Matt. 7:24-29*

Built on a Rock

Have any of you ever been in a flood? It isn't a very pretty picture, is it? The rains come down in torrents; the rivers and streams overflow their banks; and houses, lands, and people may be washed away. When it's over, the damage is almost unbelievable. (A large picture showing a devastating flood would be effective here.)

Perhaps some of you have built or helped to build your home. Remember how carefully planned it was? First, a good foundation had to be laid. Then the house was built on top of it, one board or brick at a time. Remember how you felt after the new house was completed and you moved in? What a secure feeling you had.

Then, eventually that first big storm came. The rains came down and the wind blew and beat upon the house; but when the storm was over, the house stood, because it was built on a firm foundation.

No one with any building know-how would build a house on shifting sand, would they? How foolish that would be. The house might be big and beautiful; but when the first storm came, the house would collapse into a heap of rubble because it did not have a strong foundation.

Jesus is not speaking of actually building houses in today's scriptures. He's talking about building the houses of our lives. We did not ask to be born, we just were. We build our lives one way or the other. The house or life we build is the one we must live with, also.

In America there is almost a church on every corner.

No one can say they did not have opportunity to hear the gospel. In order to become a Christian, a person needs to have at least a little knowledge of God. Knowing about Him is not enough. We must act on what we hear about God. Jesus said, "Whosoever heareth these sayings of mine, and *doeth* them, I will liken him unto a wise man." It is what we do with our knowledge of God that counts.

We probably come from many different backgrounds. Our sex, color, age, education, money or the lack of it, state of health, and what we did or do for a living may be very different, just as there are many different kinds of houses. Those things do not make any difference with God. Just as the smallest house or the largest, the humble or the elegant must all be built on a good foundation, so must our lives.

People build their lives on foundations of many things. Some have built on great wealth, now they live in poverty. Some have built on good health, and now it is failing. Others have built on fame, but it fades. Some may have built on the foundation of family, but family is all gone and they are left alone.

There is only one foundation we can build our lives on that will last when the storms come. Even the most well-ordered lives have their storms. No doubt, you have already weathered a good many of life's storms. The storms of life will crush us and leave our lives a heap of rubble unless we build on the foundation of serving Jesus Christ. God's Word tells us, "Other foundation can no man lay than that is laid, which is Jesus Christ" (1 Cor. 3:11). He is the only Foundation that will not crumble.

*   *   *

Close by praying that each one will build their lives anew on the foundation of Jesus Christ, if they have not already done so.

Scripture: *Mark 10:35-45*

Places of Honor

Remember how, as children playing together, there was always at least one who wanted to boss? If the other boys and girls got disgusted with the bossy one and went home, there was no game, because there were no players left.

This is how it is in living a Christian life. We need leaders, but they should be God-anointed, not self-appointed. Certainly, churches need leaders, but they also need followers. The minister may preach the best sermons ever, but if there is no one to listen to him, what good has been accomplished? Godly teachers are needed, but what good are they if there are no pupils to hear the lesson?

A young lady wanted to play the piano for the church choir, but that position was given to another. Instead of pouting and feeling sorry for herself, she organized a junior choir, taking much of her time and patience to teach those boys and girls to read music and count their time.

Later, when the choir pianist moved away, this girl was asked to fill that position. She had been improving her own music ability even while she taught those juniors. Now she was ready for the greater responsibility of choir pianist.

In today's scripture, James and John asked for places of honor for themselves. It was as if they were demanding, "What's in it for me?" Jesus knew that they were not ready for the places they sought. They might later obtain them, but it would be because they were ready, not because Christ loved them more than the others.

In order to become the thing of beauty as we know it, gold must be purified. In its raw state it has many impurities. That gold must be heated over an intense fire. Then all the impurities rise to the top and are skimmed off. This process is repeated over and over, until the impurities are gone, and the gold is pure and beautiful.

James and John would later be filled with the purifying fire of the Holy Spirit. They would also pass through the fires of persecution before they were ready for places of honor in God's kingdom. Eventually, James died a martyr's death. John was exiled to the Isle of Patmos. They could not have foreseen the preparation they must go through. Nothing worthwhile ever comes easy.

Perhaps none of us here have ever achieved a place of prominence. Maybe we never will in our lifetime. In the eyes of God, that doesn't matter. We can serve God with our whole hearts no matter what circumstances we find ourselves in. Life may have put us in a place of leadership for all to see and follow, or we may have only had the little-known positions. As long as we served where God wanted us, we've been in the right place.

Jesus cautions us, "Whosoever will be great among you, shall be your minister" (Mark 10:43). His idea of greatness is one who is humble enough to realize his or her own weaknesses, yet is willing to be taught at the feet of the Master Teacher of all time, Jesus Christ.

*　　*　　*

Close with prayer for each one, that they will know that in God's eyes, they are just as important as the most prominent leaders in the world.

SCRIPTURE: *Luke 2:1-16*

God's Christmas Gift to the World

(This would be a good time to have your teen carolers to sing.)

A lady was trying to buy Christmas cards in a store and finally pushed the cards aside in disgust. "Why do they have to ruin Christmastime with all this religious stuff?" It did not occur to her that without that "religious stuff" as she called it, there would be no Christmas of any kind.

Probably all of us enjoy giving and receiving gifts. Remember how, as a child, it felt so good to snuggle into a warm bed on Christmas Eve and try to imagine what gifts would be under the tree the next morning? It seemed to take forever for Christmas Day to finally arrive.

People give Christmas gifts for different reasons. Some give because they feel it's their duty. Very few people enjoy receiving a gift of that kind.

Some give to keep up appearances. A teenager had earned quite a bit of money at Christmastime and bought gifts for all of her friends. The other teens then felt they had to buy her gifts in return, to keep up appearances. They all spent more than they should have, and were unable to save any of their Christmas earnings.

Some give gifts because it's good business. A secretary in a business office received several boxes of candy for

Christmas from the business associates of her employer. There was no special joy in either the giving or receiving of the candy. It was purely for business.

Some give gifts out of habit. Two families exchanged gifts each Christmas even though they did not feel close to one another any longer. They continued to exchange gifts because it was traditional. Each one hated to be the first to break it off.

The best reason for giving gifts is because we love. This kind of giving brings joy to both the giver and the receiver. A lady with five young children received a gift from a teenage neighbor girl that she will long remember. It was simply a note reading, "For my Christmas gift to you, I promise to baby-sit three times this next year without pay. I will be available when you need me."

God enjoys giving gifts, too. On that very first Christmas Day, He gave the world the greatest Gift that has ever been or ever will be given. He gave us His only Son, Jesus Christ, who came into the world in human form as a tiny baby. (A large picture of the manger scene would be appropriate here.)

Later, Jesus would grow up and give His life on a cruel cross that we might have the gift of salvation. Isn't it marvelous that God loved us enough to offer this wonderful Gift? All we have to do is accept the Gift He has given. Let's all repeat John 3:16 together. This will remind us again of God's great Christmas Gift to all of us. (Repeat verse together.)

*　　*　　*

Close with a prayer of thanks for God's great Gift to all the world.

If you have little gifts for the patients, this would be a good time to give them.

SCRIPTURE: *2 Cor. 12:7-10*

Sufficient Grace

Bible historians tell us that Paul's thorn in the flesh was a physical disability. We don't know exactly what it was, but it bothered him quite a lot at times.

Many of you have physical disabilities of one kind or another. Some of you are in wheelchairs or even bedfast. Some may be blind or hard of hearing. Your bodies may be wracked with disease that leaves you weak and filled with pain.

Probably most of you can identify with Paul when he asked the Lord to remove his thorn in the flesh. It is not a pleasant experience to be sick or crippled, or physically handicapped in any way. We all wish to enjoy the gift of good health.

Perhaps some of you, like Paul, have prayed earnestly for the Lord to heal you, and yet your affliction remains. God does heal, but sometimes He chooses not to. Sometimes He must tell us, as He told Paul, "My grace is sufficient for thee: for my strength is made perfect in weakness."

A lady had been bedfast for better than 40 years. There had been complications at the birth of her last child, and she had been left paralyzed from the waist down. She was extremely hard of hearing, and also had arthritis so bad in her hands she was unable to straighten her fingers out.

She was a woman who had great faith in God, but He had not chosen to heal her. In place of healing, He gave her "sufficient grace." She had such a Christlike spirit that her life blessed countless others.

Even though she could not get up and about, and had to depend on others for her simplest needs, she had little time to be lonely. She fellowshiped always with her Heavenly Father. Also, she had many friends who visited her often. They would go to bring a little cheer to her life, and come away cheered themselves by her good spirit and sweet smile.

Instead of grumbling and complaining and making herself and everyone around her miserable, she allowed God to use her life to bless others. She would often clap her poor, gnarled hands together and declare, "Jesus is so good to me. He's given me so much." She had little of this world's goods, but like Paul, she had learned to glory in her infirmities, that the power of Christ would rest upon her.

Paul said, "When I am weak, then am I strong." He meant that in his human weakness, he learned to lean on the strength from God, and let His power work in Paul's life. Perhaps he was a more effective Christian because of his physical weakness. When he had prayed three times, asking God to remove his thorn in the flesh, he finally decided to leave it with the Lord.

It is not for us to decide if we will be healed physically or left with our infirmities. It is only for us to leave the whole matter with God, and let Him work out His perfect will in our lives, whatever that may be. Physical ailments will not keep us from heaven, but bitterness of soul can.

*　*　*

Pray that each one might feel God's special touch in their lives in a physical way, but even more so that they will discover God's great strength in their own weakness.